Still Marching Strong

Women in Modern America

Melissa Carosella and Stephanie Kuligowski

Consultant

Marcus McArthur, Ph.D.
Department of History
Saint Louis University

Publishing Credits

Dona Herweck Rice, *Editor-in-Chief*
Lee Aucoin, *Creative Director*
Chris McIntyre, M.A.Ed., *Editorial Director*
Torrey Maloof, *Associate Editor*
Neri Garcia, *Senior Designer*
Stephanie Reid, *Photo Researcher*
Rachelle Cracchiolo, M.A.Ed., *Publisher*

Image Credits

Teacher Created Materials

5301 Oceanus Drive
Huntington Beach, CA 92649-1030
http://www.tcmpub.com

ISBN 978-1-4333-1509-1
© 2012 by Teacher Created Materials, Inc.
BP 5028

Table of Contents

Women's Work

For centuries, women's work was limited to the home. There were strict limits on what they could do and who they could become. Those who tested the limits faced harsh **criticism**.

In the early 1900s, Eleanor Roosevelt changed the role of First Lady. She worked hard to improve the lives of others during her husband's presidency. She continued to fight for equal rights for all people after she left the White House.

In the 1920s, most of Amelia Earhart's friends were getting married. She chose to get a job and save her money for flying lessons instead. She went on to become famous for her daring **feats** of flight.

In the 1960s, Betty Friedan wondered if there was more to life than making beds and shopping. She wrote a book called *The Feminine Mystique* and helped launch a women's movement.

These women dared to be different. By breaking rules, they also broke down barriers. Their courage paved the way for the women featured in this book—and all women—to achieve their dreams.

First Lady Eleanor Roosevelt holding the Universal Declaration of Human Rights

Amelia Earhart in flight gear

Chief Wilma Mankiller

Leading a Nation

In 1985, Wilma Mankiller became the first woman elected principal chief of the Cherokee Nation. During her 10 years in office, she worked to improve the lives of her people through education and health care. In 1998, Wilma was awarded the Presidential Medal of Freedom, the highest honor for American citizens.

Playing to Win

In 1973, an aging tennis champ challenged a young female tennis star to a match. The man was 55-year-old Bobby Riggs. The woman was 29-year-old Billie Jean King. At the time, most people thought Riggs would beat Billie simply because he was a man. They were wrong. Billie easily won every set.

Billie Jean King

Women in Government

Justice for All

In 1981, Sandra Day O'Connor became the first female United States Supreme Court **justice**. U. S. President Ronald Reagan chose O'Connor because of her strong will, intelligence, and common sense.

O'Connor was born in 1930. She grew up on her family's Arizona cattle ranch. There, she learned practical skills. By age 7, she could drive a truck and brand a cow.

Madame Senator

In 1931, most women were homemakers. They cooked, cleaned, and cared for children. Hattie Caraway was like these women until her husband died suddenly. Her husband was a United States senator from Arkansas. The Arkansas governor asked Hattie to take over her husband's Senate seat.

Caraway accepted and was sworn in on December 8, 1931. In January of that year, she won a special election and became the first female elected to the United States Senate.

Justice Sandra Day O'Connor

Senator Hattie Caraway

Past and current women Supreme Court justices (from left to right): Sandra Day O'Connor, Sonia Sotomayor, Ruth Bader Ginsberg, and Elena Kagen

During every school year, O'Connor lived with her grandmother in El Paso, Texas. She attended a private girls' school where she studied hard. O'Connor was bright, and her grandmother encouraged her to excel. She graduated from high school at 16 and went on to Stanford University and Stanford Law School. She graduated third in her law school class.

O'Connor applied to many law firms, but they refused to hire a woman. She was determined to practice law, so she took a job as a county government attorney in California. Later, O'Connor moved to Arizona and worked as a state government attorney. In 1969, the governor chose her to fill an empty seat in the state senate. She was reelected to that seat twice before making history as the first female Supreme Court justice.

Powerful Public Servant

Elizabeth Hanford Dole was a natural leader at a young age. As a child, she organized games for her neighborhood playmates. In high school, she was elected class president and voted most likely to succeed. At Duke University, she served as student body president.

Dole graduated from Duke with a degree in **political science**. She then earned a **master's degree** in education from Harvard University. In 1962, she entered Harvard Law School. She was one of only 25 women in a class of 550 students. After graduation, Dole moved to Washington, DC. She wanted to work for the United States government.

Senator Elizabeth Dole

In 1996, Elizabeth Dole's husband, Robert Dole, ran for president of the United States. He lost the election to Bill Clinton.

: Representative Barbara Jordan

From Segregation to State Senate

Barbara Jordan was born in 1936 and raised in the **segregated** South. She attended all-black schools through college. Jordan went on to Boston University Law School. After graduation, she returned to Texas to practice law.

In 1966, she was elected to the Texas Senate. She made Texas history as the first African American state senator since 1883 and the first female state senator ever. In the 1970s, she served in the United States House of Representatives. Her speeches attracted national attention.

In 1975, Dole married United States Senator Robert Dole. She continued to serve in important government jobs. In the 1980s, she held two **cabinet** positions, secretary of transportation and secretary of labor. While still holding these positions, she also became president of the American Red Cross. In 2003, Dole became the first female senator from her home state of North Carolina. Dole has been called one of the most admired women in politics.

Self-Made Millionaire

Sarah Breedlove was born to freed slaves on a Louisiana plantation in 1867. She had a very tough life. The stress of her hard life caused Breedlove's hair to fall out. So, she invented a hair care product that helped her hair grow back quickly.

Breedlove changed her name to Madam C. J. Walker and sold her hair care product. Her business was a huge success. She became the first African American female millionaire.

Women in Business
Founded on Fairness

Mary Kay Ash with one of her famous pink cars

In the 1930s, Mary Kay Ash was a young wife and mother in Houston, Texas. She took a job selling cleaning supplies. She would sell the supplies to women at home parties. Her energy and charm made her a successful salesperson.

In 1952, Ash went to work for another **direct sales** company in Dallas, Texas. She came up with the idea of offering **incentives**, or prizes. These incentives made salespeople want to sell more products. Ash soon became a national training manager. But, the company kept passing her over for higher-level jobs. Instead, they gave these jobs to the men Ash had trained.

Ash quit her job and started writing a book for women in business. The book turned into a business plan for an exciting new company. Ash started her own direct sales **cosmetics** company in 1963. She promised to hire and **promote** women. Within two years, the company's sales totaled $1 million. Top sellers were rewarded with jewelry, vacations, and even pink cars!

Today, Mary Kay Inc. is one of the largest direct sellers in the world. The company has 1.8 million salespeople. Thousands of women have achieved their dreams thanks to Mary Kay Ash.

Mary Kay
cosmetics counter

Women in Activism

Keeping a Promise

Nancy Goodman Brinker made a promise to her dying sister. She vowed to stop breast cancer from killing others. Brinker's sister, Susan G. Komen (KOH-men), lost her battle with cancer in 1980 at the age of 36. But, Brinker's fight had just begun. She became an **activist**, or supporter, for the battle against breast cancer.

Brinker started a group in her home in Dallas, Texas. The group was called Susan G. Komen for the Cure. The group's mission was to end breast cancer. The members of the group worked to improve research, education, and treatment of the deadly disease.

Susan G. Komen Race for the Cure event

Nancy Goodman Brinker

Helen Keller

Paying It Forward

When Helen Keller was 19 months old, an illness left her deaf and blind. At age 7, teacher Anne Sullivan taught Keller to communicate by spelling words into her hand. Keller also learned to speak and type. In 1904, she became the first deaf-blind person to earn a college degree.

As an adult, Keller became an activist for people with disabilities. She worked to improve the lives of blind and deaf-blind people. In 1920, Keller helped start the American Civil Liberties Union. This group defends Constitutional rights.

Brinker organized fund-raising events. In 1983, she held the first Susan G. Komen Race for the Cure in Dallas. Nearly 700 people came. The next year, the group had enough money to give to hospitals and doctors for research and education.

Today, there are more than 100 Race for the Cure events held around the world every year. The foundation has raised more than $1.5 billion to fight breast cancer. In 2009, President Barack Obama awarded Brinker the Presidential Medal of Freedom for her efforts.

Opening Eyes

As a child, Rachel Carson loved spending time in nature. In 1932, she earned a master's degree in zoology. In 1962, Carson launched the modern **environmental movement** with her book *Silent Spring.* Her writing style made scientific facts interesting to everyone. In her book, she showed how **pesticides** moved from crops into soil, water, animals, and people. Carson fought for limits on the use of these dangerous chemicals.

Women in Science

On the Cutting Edge

The Jet Propulsion Laboratory (JPL), builds and runs **robotic spacecraft**. The spacecraft JPL designs are used by the National Aeronautics and Space Administration (NASA). JPL built and launched America's first **satellite** in 1958. Today, JPL has more than 20 spacecraft exploring the galaxy.

Claudia Alexander is pushing the limits of space exploration. She is a scientist at JPL. She started working there in 1986. She worked on the Galileo (gal-uh-LEY-oh) mission. This mission sent a satellite to study Jupiter and its moons.

Alexander discovered her interest in space during high school. She was chosen for a summer job at a research center at NASA. She often snuck into the **planetary science** department to check out the experiments. This led her to study **geophysics** in college. Geophysics is a science that deals with the physical processes that happen on or near Earth. Alexander went on to earn top degrees in different branches of geophysics.

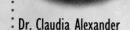

Dr. Claudia Alexander

These images of Jupiter and its four moons were taken by the Galileo spacecraft.

The Galileo spacecraft

Alexander has studied comets, solar wind, Venus, and Jupiter and its moons. In 2003, she received the Emerald Honor for Women of Color in Research and Engineering. And in 2005, she earned the NASA leadership medal.

Women in Photojournalism

Camera Ready

Lynsey Addario

Lynsey Addario travels the world with her camera in hand. Through the camera lens, she captures truths about people's lives. Addario is a **photojournalist**. She takes pictures for a living. Her pictures have been published in *National Geographic* and *Time Magazine*.

Addario (second from left) was captured shortly after this picture was taken in Libya.

In 1995, Addario graduated from the University of Wisconsin-Madison. Her degree is in world relations and Italian. She had no photography training, but she began working as a newspaper photographer the very next year.

Addario has covered events in Iraq, Lebanon, Darfur, and Congo. She heads into war zones and countries in crisis. She does this to tell stories about the people affected by these events. Her pictures bring awareness to important global issues and the treatment of women.

Dorothea Lange

Photographing the Great Depression

Dorothea Lange was a photographer in San Francisco, California, during the Great Depression. One day, she took her camera out of the studio and into the streets. She photographed people waiting in a bread line. The powerful images changed Lange's life.

From that day on, Lange photographed events in American history. She is most famous for her photos of poor farm families during the Great Depression. Lange's photos brought their struggles to the attention of the world.

In 2009, Addario was part of the team that won a Pulitzer Prize for International Reporting. In 2010, Oprah Winfrey named Addario as one of 20 women on her Power List.

Addario's work is exciting but dangerous. In March 2011, she was one of four journalists captured during a conflict in Libya. She was held captive for nearly six days.

A Style of Her Own

Georgia O'Keeffe was born in Wisconsin in 1887. During childhood art lessons, her artistic talent became clear. She dreamed of becoming an artist.

As an adult, O'Keeffe found her own unique style of abstract art. This means that she painted objects she found in nature the way she wanted to, rather than exactly how they looked. She used bold colors in her abstract paintings.

By 1918, Georgia's dream had come true. She was a professional painter on the way to becoming one of America's greatest artists.

Women in Art

Visionary Designer

Maya Lin is an artist and an **architect**. Her designs make people think. Her buildings, **memorials**, and sculptures are both beautiful and full of meaning. She uses natural materials such as water, rock, and soil to tell a story.

As a student at Yale University, Lin entered a competition to design a Vietnam Veterans Memorial. Over 1,000 people entered the contest. Her design won. Her design is a V-shaped wall of black **granite**. It lists the names of more than 58,000 American soldiers killed in the war. The Wall, as it is known, was built in Washington, DC, in 1982. Today, it is the most visited memorial in the nation's capital.

Maya Lin

...UNTIL JUSTICE ROLLS DOWN LIKE WATERS
AND RIGHTEOUSNESS LIKE A MIGHTY STREAM.

MARTIN LUTHER KING, JR.

Civil Rights Memorial
in Alabama

Vietnam Veterans
Memorial in
Washington, DC

In 1986, Lin graduated from Yale University with a master's degree in architecture. She went on to design many public memorials and buildings. Her designs include the Civil Rights Memorial in Alabama and the Museum of Chinese in America in New York City. Her most recent project is called *What Is Missing?* It pays tribute to plants, animals, and places that are, or will soon be, **extinct**. In 2009, President Barack Obama awarded Lin the National Medal of Arts.

Women in Literature

From World Travel to Time Travel

Mary Pope Osborne signs a book for a young fan

Mary Pope Osborne grew up in a military family and had to move often. She did not mind because each new place stretched her imagination. In Austria, the castle on a nearby cliff brought the magic of fairy tales right into her neighborhood. In Virginia, living in an old fort transported her back in time. In North Carolina, a community theater let her explore characters on stage.

MAGIC TREE HOUSE #31
A MERLIN MISSION
Summer of the Sea Serpent
Mary Pope Osborne

A book from the Magic Tree House series

Beverly Cleary

Giving Kids What They Want

As a child, Beverly Cleary loved to read. But, she had trouble finding stories to which she could relate. Cleary's school librarian told her that she should write books for children someday. Cleary liked that idea. She wanted to write funny stories with characters like her.

Cleary grew up to be an award-winning author of many children's books that have become **classics**. She writes books that reflect kids' lives. Cleary's more memorable characters include Ramona Quimby and Ralph S. Mouse.

After graduating from college, Osborne did not settle down. She set out to explore the world. She camped in a cave on the island of Crete, survived an earthquake in Afghanistan, and got blood poisoning in Nepal. These real-life adventures were put to good use when Osborne discovered her talent for writing fiction.

In 1982, Osborne published her first book for young readers. It was called *Run, Run as Fast as You Can*. It told the story of a girl from a military family. In 1992, she published *Dinosaurs Before Dark*. It was the first book in the Magic Tree House series. With their simple plots and exciting use of time travel, the books have inspired millions of kids to read chapter books.

Speaking Kids' Language

Judy Blume changed the world of young adult fiction. She wrote about the lives of children and teens with honesty and humor.

For more than 40 years, Blume has written stories that spoke to kids. Her books include such hits as *Freckle Juice* and the Fudge series. Her books have helped generations of readers feel less alone with their problems.

Collins holds one of her books

Trusting Young Readers

When best-selling author Suzanne Collins was in elementary school, her English teacher read Edgar Allen Poe stories to the class. Collins loved the grown-up tales of mystery and horror. She was also impressed that her teacher thought she was old enough for stories like "The Telltale Heart."

As a writer, Collins also trusts young readers with grown-up subject matter. Her action-packed Underland Chronicles series deals with loss, war, and a **plague** (pleyg). Her popular Hunger Games trilogy is about a **futuristic** society. The characters struggle with an unfair government, poverty, and violence.

Collins's subject matter is serious, but she believes young people should think about life's big issues. Her readers enjoy the challenge. They also love her fast-paced plots and realistic characters. Readers often say they cannot put Collins's books down because they *have* to know what happens next. For Collins, the best praise is hearing that kids who usually do not like to read, love reading her books!

Collins's famous books

Women in Entertainment

Changing the World

Oprah Winfrey has made her mark on every aspect of the entertainment world. She had the most successful television talk show of all time. She has starred in movies. And, she owns a magazine and cable television network called OWN (Oprah Winfrey Network). Winfrey is often called the most powerful woman in the world.

In 1984, Winfrey was a television news anchor hired to save a failing morning show in Chicago. She not only saved the show, but she turned it into the most popular show in town. The next year, it was renamed *The Oprah Winfrey Show*. In 1986, it was broadcast nationally and quickly became the number one talk show in America.

Oprah Winfrey

Oprah Winfrey in the movie *The Color Purple*

Barbara Walters

First Female News Anchor

Barbara Walters is famous for her work as a serious journalist and a respected talk-show host. She has interviewed the world's most powerful leaders and famous celebrities.

In 1974, Walters became the first female co-host of a morning news broadcast called *The Today Show*. In 1976, she became the first female co-anchor of an evening news broadcast. In recent years, she has been a host on *The View*, a show she created and produces.

Winfrey interviews President Obama and First Lady Michelle Obama on her talk show.

In the 1990s, Winfrey began to focus on helping people. She featured health, exercise, and spiritual ideas on her show. She promoted the work of professionals in other fields. She soon became a billionaire and shared her wealth generously. She has given more than $50 million to charity.

Sliding Into Home (with Style)

In the fall of 1942, American baseball had a problem. Young men were being drafted for World War II. Minor league teams were losing players. So, Phillip Wrigley, owner of the Chicago Cubs, decided to start a women's softball league. He hoped the women's teams would fill the baseball stadiums.

The women practiced hard all day. At night, they attended classes on manners. They were expected to be athletic and charming.

The All-American Girls Professional Baseball League opened doors for women athletes. From 1943 to 1954, about 600 women played professional sports for the first time.

Women in Sports
Winning Streak

Unbeatable. Record-breaking. Perfect. These words describe the University of Connecticut women's basketball team during three amazing seasons from 2008 to 2010. The team is known as the UConn Huskies, and they dominated the sport with a 90-game winning streak. The streak broke the record of 88 games won in a row. During the streak, UConn beat the other teams by an average of 33 points.

All-American Girls Professional Baseball players in action

The UConn team with President Obama

The secret to their success was not a secret at all. Some of the most talented players in the sport had come together at UConn. Maya Moore was the best forward. Tina Charles was the best center. And Renee Montgomery was the best point guard. The players mastered the art of teamwork, and they played with a strong sense of purpose.

The winning streak was exciting, but the team's goal was always to be the best team in the nation. They achieved that goal by winning the National Collegiate Athletic Association (NCAA) women's basketball championship in 2010.

The UConn Huskies make the cover of *Sports Illustrated*.

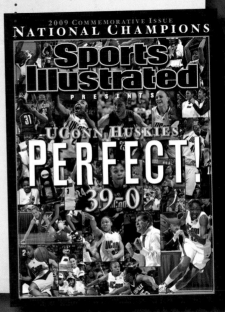

Dreams Come True

At one time in America, a woman's place was in the home. Women's work was cooking, cleaning, and raising children. Women who wanted to pursue careers outside the home faced great challenges.

Today, women work in a variety of professions. Women can make laws, run companies, or build robotic spacecraft. Others design buildings or interview world leaders. There are countless women, whose names are not famous, that make a difference every day as teachers, engineers, doctors, accountants, construction workers, and computer scientists. These days, women's career choices are limited only by their imaginations.

When the Founding Fathers were drafting the United States Constitution, Abigail Adams asked her husband, John Adams, to "remember the ladies." At first, women were not written into the Constitution. They were not given equal rights. They had to fight and work hard to achieve equality. But, they did it. The strong will and determination of these women will be remembered.

Leaders of tomorrow